LINDA BROWN,

YOU ARE NOT ALONE

The Brown

v.

Board of

Education Decision

A Collection Edited by

JOYCE CAROL THOMAS

Illustrations by

CURTIS JAMES

JUMP AT THE SUN
HYPERION BOOKS FOR CHILDREN
NEW YORK

Printed in Singapore
First Edition
1 3 5 7 9 10 8 6 4 2

Designed by Christine Kettner
This book is set in 14.5-point Mrs. Eaves.
Library of Congress Cataloging-in-Publication Data on file.
ISBN 0-7868-0821-7 (tr. ed.)
ISBN 0-7868-2640-1 (lib. ed.)
Visit www.hyperionchildrensbooks.com

I thank executive editor Maureen Sullivan for her
steadfast support.

For imagining the possibilities of this anthology, I thank
Andrea Pinkney.

For naming this anthology and continuing the vision,
I thank Lisa Holton.

For her impeccable design and powerful touch spread
throughout this collection, I thank Christine Kettner.

I thank Anna Ghosh, my resolute, diligent agent.

To the black and white authors gathered here who
answered my call for their remembered experiences and
stories surrounding the 1954 Supreme Court decision,
my respectful appreciation.

And last, but not least, to Curtis James,
the artist who offers his paintings inspired by this
fifty-year American anniversary, my everlasting gratitude.

To my son, Michael A. Withers
—J.C.T.

To my brothers and sisters,
Edna, Willie, Thelma, Loretta, Alva, Lillie, Bobby,
and Anthony,
and to Linda Brown
and all those who experienced desegregation in America
—C.E.J.

CONTENTS

WHO IS
LINDA BROWN?

by Joyce Carol Thomas

As EARLY AS 1896, it was legal to separate blacks and whites, as long as facilities, such as water fountains, lunch counters, movie theaters, and schools, were "equal." This concept is called *segregation*.

In Topeka, Kansas, fifty-four years ago, Reverend Oliver L. Brown escorted his eight-year-old daughter Linda to the all-white Sumner Elementary School, located a short four blocks from their front door. Although Reverend Brown appealed to the Sumner Elementary School principal to let him register Linda, he and his daughter were denied access and turned away.

Subsequently, Linda Brown attended the segregated black Monroe Elementary School. It is important to note that more teachers at Monroe Elementary held master of Education degrees than did teachers at the all-white Sumner Elementary School. In addition, the same construction company had built both school facilities. Reverend Brown's concern was not the competence of the Monroe faculty or the quality of the building. He wanted equal access to the school nearest his home. His concern was that his young daughter had to walk along dangerous railroad tracks through weather that sometimes turned icy and stormy to get to Monroe Elementary. Many children like Linda Brown had to walk miles to school and sometimes wait at the bus stop to be carried even farther from home.

Urged on by the NAACP, Reverend Brown and twelve more African American families filed a lawsuit for equal access. They petitioned the Kansas Board of Education on behalf of their children.

As Linda Brown's sister, Cheryl Brown Henderson, reminds us, the Kansas lawsuit that was named after their father; also, we understand that the majority of the challengers for equal access were African American mothers. Kansas was not the only state involved. The group of states challenging the "separate but equal" principle included Delaware, South Carolina, Virginia, and the District of Columbia. The equal-access petition fought for Linda and more than one hundred other children.

On May 17, 1954, after considering the facts of the Brown case, the Supreme Court held that public institutions, including schools, would no longer be allowed to segregate people based on their skin color. Yet twenty-five years later, in 1979, a group of young attorneys, fearing resegregation, had to petition the federal court to press on with the fight for equal access.

The 1954 *Brown v. Board of Education* unanimous decision, which deemed segregation unlawful in twenty other states besides Kansas, did not stop segregation. Many black schools remained dilapidated shacks with tattered books and outhouses.

Did Linda Brown Thompson give up? Apparently not, for in 1984, thirty years after the Supreme Court Decision, she said, "It's disheartening that we are still fighting." In Topeka, Kansas, where she still lived, the segregation of black and white students persisted.

Eventually, Monroe Schools built three racially balanced magnet schools with excellent teaching programs. This brings us to another question about equal access. Did the educational system ever change for the better? In one of grandmother Linda Brown Thompson's interviews, she says, "There is still a lot of work to be done." Fifty years later, many schools are not only still segregated but those that were integrated are now *re*segregating.

Perhaps the assumption was that if the doors were open to black children, educators would care for both black and white children, yet we find that underprepared schoolteachers, administrators, and the society around many failing school districts don't care enough about black children or their educational development. Although segregation remains illegal in the workplace, housing, and education, many believe that segregation now may actually be more destructive than it was in 1956.

During this fifty-year commemoration of the Brown decision, Linda Brown Thompson and all the children who suffered in their journey continue to champion equal access.

INTRODUCTION

ONCE UPON A TIME, on the other side of freedom, dawn waved across a field to awaken a field hand and his daughter. In dawn's glow, the dark farmer lowered his dusty straw hat over his brow. He plowed clods of hard dirt into furrows of yielding earth.

Around noon he was ready for lunch and his *prize*. His prize? It was not just the dipper of ice-cold water that his young daughter handed him. He swallowed the cool drink in glad gulps. The prize was not just the fragrant offering in the lunch basket. His child pulled away two cotton napkins covering the baked yams, biscuits, fried chicken, peppergrass

greens, and blackstrap molasses. They feasted in silence.

Appetite answered, now farmer and daughter stood and moved toward the waiting prize. Where was this prize, so anticipated? They found it hidden beneath a mulberry bush. The farmer sat under the shady arbor and held one arm around his child. His work-hardened fingers opened a book, a blue-back *Webster's*.

His weary voice sounded out the letters above the crackle of the pages.

His daughter echoed the syllables until they sang. Then she whispered entire words.

Look! See how the thirsty minds of the farmer and his daughter were quenched on the other side of freedom a full century before. The awakening toward learning continued.

In looking back, even as you move forward, you might wonder, Who were these Americans who troubled the waters to uphold ideals in the 1950s?

They were articulate and extraordinary blacks.

They were articulate in their poems, sermons, songs, and speeches. Extraordinary in their paintings, sculptures, dances.

Preachers in pulpits, poets at their podiums,

writers at their desks, artists before their easels, composers with their instruments—all contributed in their distinct ways.

Bankers, maids, lawyers, Pullman porters, housewives, and cotton pickers welcomed tired and hungry protesters into their homes. They gave them tin cups brimming with water and offered them beds and bowls of food.

And the young people? Perhaps they were the most articulate and extraordinary of all. They walked quietly and bravely through storm and rain to the front lines of freedom. One of them was Linda Brown.

In the passion of battle, shortsighted whites didn't care that Linda Brown had to travel a long and dangerous route to school each day while many other black children shivered in winter's unheated rooms, where science texts and mildewed math books had pages missing.

Mean-spirited grown-ups brawled in the streets to keep a high wall around their neat buildings. They hurled rocks to protect Mississippi cities from girls in pigtails. And girls in neat bobby socks with books tucked under their trembling arms waded through hate.

Louisiana whites carried "Go back to Africa!" signs and turned fire hoses on clean-cut boys in bow ties. Black parents walked through trouble as though they were sure God would hear their cries, their prayers.

Some white parents and legislators fought change by standing in schoolhouse doors to block any black child who dared cross the threshold. And white segregationists had the audacity to broadcast their backward ways in court chambers.

But their objections, no matter how powerful, were not strong enough to stop a righteous cause. Bold, determined blacks took to Alabama streets and country back roads. Marched. Argued before Arkansas judges for a new legacy.

African Americans surged forward, singing, "Just like a tree planted by the water / We shall not be moved."

They sang as if they knew that a tree planted by the water would prosper, for its roots drank in life-giving moisture.

Well, eventually, whites followed African Americans in their thirst for justice.

Over time, fairness began to win out in Topeka, Kansas; in Mississippi; in Louisiana; in Georgia; in border states, as well as in western and northern states as far apart as California and New York.

It seems as if everybody took hope. As if everybody took hold.

The souls of black people sang, "Yes." When white people of goodwill listened to them, the soul of America echoed, "Yes." And white children, who were also listening and watching, were ushered into a new awakening.

Together blacks and whites worked toward the triumph of *Brown v. Board of Education*. We were building then. And we are still building.

You may want to think about what the "United" in the United States of America means. The 1954 decision, ignited by the earlier and later demands of Linda Brown's father, united us and moved this country toward a more democratic future, toward a true uniting of states.

With the 9–0 decision in the *Brown v. Board of Education* case, the Supreme Court followed the unified will of a unified people. And the future for you became clearer.

Fifty years later, does the African American inspired concept of justice still shine a beacon from the Pacific to the Atlantic? Do we still see it?

To commemorate this extraordinary anniversary, I invited my fellow children's book writers who were all young people themselves at the time of the decision to recall their personal experiences. Their recollections capture a small slice of a remarkable moment in history.

Many questions may arise in your mind. Some of these will be answered when you read Eloise Greenfield's memorable poem, "Desegregation," which centers on the concerns of black children. Her poetry is followed by her poignant and thoughtful essay, "Legacy."

Do you want to know about a drum major who rallied for a more wholesome America? Katherine Paterson's splendid and heartbreakingly honest "The Prophet" tells of just such a person who was once as young as you. His name? Martin Luther King, Jr.

In Ishmael Reed's "Color Blind," we witness his genius and clear-eyed analysis at work. His essay chronicles what he sees as the breaking down of the black community brought on by desegregation. He tells us what the *Brown* decision means to him.

Lois Lowry's breathtaking and powerful "Anthony" will make you happy at times and sad at other times. And Jean Craighead George's compassionate and compelling "The Awakening" asks you to look deeper at all that goes on around you in this great nation.

Quincy Troupe expresses his memories in his eloquent "St. Louis," with its unforgettable anger and lists of outrages. His essay invites you inside his world to glimpse the treacherous journey of his youth.

Jerry Spinelli's astounding "Wonamona," in delighting you with the perils and joys of childhoods over half a century ago, will have an impact that is at once present and timeless.

In Leona Welch's triumphant short story, "My Dear Colored People," her aching remembrance strikes at the bone of what blacks have suffered and loved their way through.

Michael Cart, in his touching, personal, and provocative essay, "Mike and Me," provides library lessons about the kinds of books you would have missed back then and the ones you enjoy now.

"Stormy Weather" sparked my memory. I followed threads of painful events in celebrating the unforgettable triumph of what happened to Mama and me on the road to Oklahoma.

So, dear reader, we come to reflect, to rejoice, and to consider how much farther we have to go.

Today, the *Brown* victory is still leading all of America's children, including all of you now turning these pages, into the twenty-first century and beyond.

We thank Linda Brown. We thank the brave children of our past. We are mindful that some of those brave children, who are now adults, still bear the scars of that battle.

Although you may not have a blue-black *Webster's*, your books can be just as exciting. Your thirst is the same as that of the child who wanted her father to read to her under the mulberry bush. Can you hear her singing syllables into words because she wanted to read books for herself?

As we celebrate the fifty-year milestone of the *Brown* decision we—your authors, illustrators, librarians, teachers, and parents—applaud your belief in education for all. Let us continue to work toward true democracy.

Joyce Carol Thomas

LINDA BROWN,

YOU ARE NOT ALONE

The Brown

v.

Board of

Education Decision

WONAMONA
by Jerry Spinelli

R EYBURN COPPERWELL was the color of a Hershey bar. One day, to prove it, we each kicked in a nickel and bought one. He unwrapped it. He put it next to his arm. The colors matched perfectly. "See," he said, "you can't even tell which is which." He held out his arm. "They even taste the same. Take a bite." I did. I bit harder than either of us expected. He yowled. We laughed.

I was the white one. Still am, though I have yet to find a candy bar or anything else on earth that exactly matches me.

Reyburn liked to put on airs. He used to say, "My grandpa was a chief in Africa."

I told him, "Reyburn, knock it off. Your grandpa wasn't no chief nowhere. Your grandpa is a cook at the Gateway Diner."

At that point he always changed the subject, until the day he didn't. He said, "My African name is Wonamona. Call me Wonamona."

"I'll call you Wonapoopee," I said.

He tried to keep a straight face, but couldn't. We laughed a lot.

But he wouldn't let it go. In those days when we went to each other's house, we didn't knock on the front door or ring the bell. We just stood on the sidewalk and called:

"Yo, Reyburn!"

"Yo, Albie!"

Except now it had to be "Yo, Wonamona!"

"Or Wonamona won't come out," he said.

I was not about to play along with such nonsense. Next morning, I went with the usual: "Yo, Reyburn!" He didn't come out. I knew he was bluffing. I kept calling. He kept not coming out. Not even a peeking eyeball in the window. The sidewalk was heating up. Usually we were far from our houses by now.

Okay, I thought, *you want to play that game.* I walked

away, down to my house, turned. His door was still shut. I had my pride. I went in. I sat by the front window. A hundred times I heard him call, "Yo, Albie!" But always only in my ears.

Finally after dinner I took pity on him, decided to give him another chance. I went to his house.

"Yo, Reyburn!"

Nothing.

"Yo, Reyburn!"

In a world of doors, his was the shuttest.

I ran home. I kicked my bed. I left him out of my prayers. Next morning, I was there as the fathers headed off to work. I didn't plan it. I just opened my mouth and let come out whatever was in there.

"Yo, Wonamona!"

The door opened.

We laughed. He flew from the steps and we gave each other strangleholds and fell to the ground.

I went back to calling him Reyburn. I figured: *That's it. He got it out of his system. We're done with the Africa stuff.* But he was just getting started.

A few days later he came to his door in a sheet. It was wrapped around him so that one shoulder showed. And bare Hershey-bar feet. There were green and yellow paint splotches all over the sheet.

His skin had never looked browner.

He looked down at me from the top step. His face was stern. He held up one hand, palm to the street, as if he were taking an oath. "Yo," he said. "Wonamona greets you."

I cracked up. "You're so dumb," I told him. "That's what Indians do. You don't even know how to act like an African."

"Wonamona greets you," he repeated. Low-voiced monotone.

"I ain't calling you Wonamona no more."

And I didn't. But he wore that sheet robe around the neighborhood all day long. Every time he came to a grown-up, up went the hand: "Wonamona greets you."

This was 1954, the summer before fifth grade. As you can tell, Reyburn Copperwell was ahead of his time. I just figured he was goofy.

You probably think we had been friends forever, but the fact is we had met only that summer. He had moved into a house at the other end of my block, and the next day our bikes crashed in the alley. As we picked ourselves up, I noticed he was wearing a gimp bracelet, like me. I pointed to it. "You make that?"

"Yeah," he said.

His strands of braided gimp were red and yellow; mine were blue and white. Then I saw the baseball cards woven into the spokes of his front wheel.

"Got a lotta cards?" I said.

"Two hundred and seven."

I whistled. I only had a hundred and fifty-eight. "Bob Feller?" I said.

"Five," he said.

Impressive, but not shocking. Everybody had multiple Bob Fellers. But there was one card I coveted above all others, and I couldn't find it anywhere. "Cookie Lavagetto?"

"One."

I almost fainted. "Where'd you get it?"

"Flipped a kid for it."

"How many flippers you got?"

He looked at me like I was crazy. "All of 'em," he said.

I gawked at him. I knew right then that this kid was different. Flippers were the cards you used in flipping contests, the cards you were willing to risk losing. Risking all of your cards was unheard of.

"The Lavagetto?" I said. I could hardly breathe.

He grinned. He nodded.

We rode off to his house.

We flipped cards in his backyard for hours. I kept waiting for the Lavagetto to show up. Finally, I said, "Where's the Lavagetto?"

He took one off the bottom of his stack. "You mean this?"

"Flip it," I said. "C'mon."

"Tomorrow."

"You said they're all flippers."

He waved it under my nose, let me smell it. I swore if I ever won it from him it would never leave my hands for the rest of my life.

He grinned. "Tomorrow."

That night I told my parents a colored family had moved in down the street.

"No they didn't," said my mother.

"Yes they did," I said. "I played with the kid. His name's Reyburn."

"No they didn't," she said.

So I guess it was a ghost I played with all summer.

We made gimp bracelets and belts and straps to hang our penknives from. We inspected the gutters and sewers for interesting stuff. We made fans from Popsicle sticks. We shot marbles. We played chew-the-peg and Old Maid and bombed the flower-bed slugs, shouting "Hockers away!" We rode our bikes and hunted garter snakes and shared glass quart bottles of strawberry milk. We made a tree hole our secret place and left notes for each other there.

We flipped cards every day. Every day he waved the Cookie Lavagetto under my nose and said, "Tomorrow."

Finally, I snapped. "You said that yesterday. This *is* tomorrow."

He grinned. "Tomorrow."

"You're a dirty liar, Reyburn, you know that? You said they were all flippers."

He kissed the card and returned it to the bottom of the deck.

"Tomorrow."

"Liar."

Sometimes he laughed me off. Sometimes he got a hurt look on his face, as if his own lie were causing him pain. In spite of my own two eyes and my own good sense, all summer long he made me believe that tomorrow would actually come. It was years before I could see that I was being bribed with a promise.

There were many things I didn't see that summer. I didn't see that Mrs. Copperwell was always painting over words that appeared on her front door. I thought she was just crazy about painting.

I didn't see that after the first week or two of living on our block, Mr. Copperwell took to parking his car in another part of town.

I didn't see that it was always Reyburn and me— and nobody else.

And I didn't see that Reyburn's hair was getting longer and longer, until I called up for him one day late in August. He came to the door and up went the hand. "Wonamona greets you."

Oh no, I thought.

But what really got my attention was his hair. It was sticking straight up, as if he had put his finger in an electric socket. This was before Afros and Don King.

"What happened to your hair?" I said.

"It's my natural hair," he said. "When I go back to Africa I got to be ready."

By the next day his mother had put a stop to that. I heard her yelling at him inside the house. So Reyburn started bringing a comb with him, and once we were out of range he got that hair standing up straight as Popsicle sticks.

And that's how we went to school first day, fifth

grade. I was feeling embarrassed, but I tried not to show it. When the teacher called out his name, he said, "Wonamona here." I shrank back into my chair. The teacher looked from the roll book to him and back again and went on to the next kid.

Even the other colored kids kept their distance at first, as if he were a different species. And when he said "Wonamona greets you" to them, they looked at each other funny and crinkled their faces as if they had just gotten a whiff of something they expected to smell bad once they took a deep breath.

But leave it to Reyburn, he was just so doggone friendly that within a week or two he had all of those crinkles smoothed out. The colored kids never did call him Wonamona, but some of the white kids did. When they saw him coming, they didn't even wait for him to say it. Shouts flew across the school yard: "Yo, Wonamona!" Some of them couldn't say it often enough. It tickled them like forty feathers.

Of course, these were fifth graders. Sixth graders, that was another story.

When I first caught him saying "Wonamona greets you" to a sixth grader, the kid cursed at Reyburn and shoved him backward.

"Reyburn," I said, "that was a sixth grader. Don't

mess with them. And don't even *look* at junior high kids."

"Who's messin'?" he said. "I'm just being me."

"Take my advice," I told him. "With sixth graders, be somebody else."

Naturally, he didn't stop talking to sixth graders any more than his hair stopped growing. By Halloween, it looked a foot tall. One day, after combing it up on the way to school, he left the comb sticking right there, in his hair. From then on he always wore it that way.

I could have told him what would happen next, and it did. A sixth grader walked clear across the school yard, walked right up to Reyburn, yanked the comb from his hair and snapped it in two. He threw the pieces at Reyburn's feet. Reyburn held up his hand. "Wonamona greets you."

The kid laughed and walked away.

Next day there was a new comb in Reyburn's hair, plus two pencils. The sixth grader came over and did the same thing.

"Wonamona greets you."

This time the sixth grader didn't laugh. This time he said, "Greet this, jigaboo," and he busted Reyburn in the face.

I don't know what I expected, but I remember the first thought that skipped across my brain: *He doesn't bleed Hershey bars*. He wouldn't stop bleeding, and he wouldn't cry. He just started walking away. I went with him. I couldn't believe I was walking away from school during recess.

Neither of us had a hankie. Grown-ups stared at us. I kept holding the sleeve of my jacket under his nose to stop the blood. He kept pushing it away. He said nothing. When we got to his house, he stumbled up the steps and went inside.

The next day, for the first time, I saw the words on their front door. I called, "Yo, Reyburn!" Then "Yo, Wonamona!" I kept calling, as if calling it could make him appear. But even then I think I knew I would never see him again.

Snow was on the ground when, for some reason, it occurred to me to check on the secret place. I went to the tree hole and reached in. I felt something. I pulled it out. All I could do was stand there like a dummy and stare. It was the card. The Cookie Lavagetto.

JERRY SPINELLI received the Newbery Medal for *Maniac Magee*. Among his many other books for children are *Stargirl* and *Loser*.

DESEGREGATION

by Eloise Greenfield

We walk the long path
lined with shouting
nightmare faces,
nightmare voices.
Inside the school,
there are eyes that glare
and eyes that are distant.
We wish for our friends.
We wish for our old,
laughing selves.
We hold our heads up,
hold our tears in.
The grown-ups have said
we must be brave,
that only the children
can save the country
now.

LEGACY
by Eloise Greenfield

I T H A P P E N E D on my twenty-fifth birth-
day. I remember the exact moment that I heard the
decision. It was after lunch, and I was working at my
job at the United States Patent Office when an
African American coworker burst into the room
with the news. At first, I laughed. I was surprised and
happy. But then I forced myself to straighten my
face, because I noticed that the room suddenly had
become quiet and tense. The office remained that
way the rest of the day.

Division Eight of the Patent Office occupied
four or five adjoining rooms of the Department of
Commerce building in Washington, D.C. In my

room there were three of us, all women—an African American file clerk, a white clerical supervisor, and myself. I was a clerk-typist. In the other rooms were men, maybe eleven or twelve of them, all white except one. They were the professional staff. Called examiners, they studied each patent application to decide whether it met the standards necessary to be called an invention.

On a normal day, there was a fair amount of chatting and laughter among the employees as we moved back and forth through the rooms doing our work. But on the afternoon of May 17, 1954, the mood was different. There was anger in some of the faces. In others, there was a kind of discomfort, which I interpreted as attempts to walk the middle ground, to hide which side they were on. I didn't know what was being said in the other rooms when I was at my desk or when the other two African Americans were out of earshot, but I could sense that it wasn't pleasant.

Racial discrimination has no logic. It doesn't make sense. That's why the same rules didn't apply in every town. African Americans, when they traveled, had to find out in each place they went what they could and could not do. In some places, for example, public transportation was segregated, but in Washington, D.C., where I grew up in the nineteen thirties and forties, it was not. We were barred from many theaters, restaurants, and drugstore soda fountains, but we could sit anywhere on streetcars.

When I was a teenager, I rode the streetcar to high school every day. I sat beside white passengers only when there was no other seat. Usually, when I did, he or she would squeeze closer to the window, or jump up and angrily brush past me. I was always glad when a passenger chose to jump up, because then one of my friends could come and sit beside me. My parents, by their attitude, had taught me to place the burden of racism where it belonged, and so I never thought there was anything wrong with me. There was something wrong with the person who had been rude.

Growing up, I seldom felt directly, person to person, the ugliness of racism, although, of course, many adults felt it daily, especially at work. But in Washington, we lived mostly in our own part of the city, and my contacts with others were occasional and fleeting.

In our part of the city, as seen through my child's eyes, we had just about everything we

needed—attractive theaters, restaurants, soda fountains, newspapers, churches, schools, and much
more. And there was the beautiful Howard
University campus I loved to walk through. Howard
had a junior music school, where one of my friends
studied piano. Another friend, Merion, studied
violin there, and her mother allowed me to come
along and watch the lessons being taught by world-
famous African American violinist Louia Vaughn
Jones.

For both African Americans and whites, the
economic levels of Washington residents ranged
from wealth to middle income to low income to
poverty. My family fell into the third group. We
didn't have very many extras, and what we did have
couldn't be wasted, but there was always enough. We
lived in neat, working-class neighborhoods.

When I was nine years old, we moved to
Langston Terrace, a new low-rent housing project,
one of the first in the country. The project was
surrounded mostly by African American
homeowners, who became our friends. Most of us
who lived in Langston Terrace still love the memory
of it. We have had reunions where almost a hundred
of us gathered and celebrated growing up there.

Our schools were large, brick buildings. Some were fairly recently built with the kinds of windows that allowed sufficient light to enter. Others were many years old and not as bright. Everyone in the schools was African American, all the principals, all the teachers, and all the students. We had good teachers (with some exceptions) who cared about us and wanted us to have great futures. They told us to reach for the stars.

We loved our schools. At least, we loved them as much as children can love a place that gives them homework. But it was an atmosphere that made us happy, encouraged us to learn, and gave us our school spirit. *Proud* was a word we used often.

At Cardozo High School, we admired the vale-dictorians, cheered for the athletes, and proudly wore our school colors, purple and white.

In junior high school, we sang, "Browne Junior High so brave, so strong, Oh, Browne Junior High so proud!" and meant it. Once, the teachers at Browne performed in a play, with us, the students, as the audience. In another play, *The Pied Piper of Hamelin*, I was one of the children that the piper led away from home.

The elementary schools I attended also have

special meaning for me. In the spring of 2002, I made an author visit to Charles Young Elementary School, which I attended in fifth and sixth grades. When I mentioned to a childhood friend that I was going, she wanted to go, and I was glad to have her with me. Much had changed at the school in the sixty-two years since we graduated, but the photograph we had been proud of, African American Colonel Charles Young, still hung there, and the auditorium looked almost the same. The students welcomed me with a WELCOME HOME, ELOISE GREENFIELD banner stretched across the stage. I was happy to be home.

My parents had the same pride in the schools they attended in the little town of Parmele, North Carolina, in the early part of the twentieth century. Their teachers had high standards, requiring the students to master English, Latin, math, science, history, and other subjects. My parents studied African American history years before Carter G. Woodson, in 1926, began the annual observation of Negro History Week.

As a child, I never saw the inside of a white school. I didn't know until later that they had better science laboratories and other equipment than our schools. But I did know that the city government allotted less money to us. Often, needed repairs on our buildings were not made for months or years, and while there were more than enough schools for white children, we had too few. Some of their schools were not nearly filled to capacity, and at least one was half-empty. Many of ours were overcrowded.

Sometimes, in my schools, there was not enough paper and other materials to go around. My pet peeve, though, was that our "new" books were actually old books with frayed covers, sent to us after the white schools had worn them out and replaced them. Some of us complained among ourselves. The schools were supported by our families' taxes, and it was angering to know that the money was being spent unfairly.

At the time, however, these problems all felt like minor inconveniences. The overwhelming reality of my school life was the strength I found there, the learning, the nurturing, and the fun.

The details of history are dependent on time and place. In some places and at some times, there were devastating and drastic differences between the two school systems, white and black. Children had to walk long distances in extremely hot or cold weather to schools that could not provide buses, or they suffered and became ill in schools that had too little money to maintain heat in the winter. Education had to take place in institutions that were not just uncomfortable and difficult, but dangerous, and although many learned because of their courage and the dedication of their teachers, others were lost along the way.

With desegregation came other problems, however. In some schools, African American students are still not being graded fairly or given access to advanced classes. Parents, community groups, and organizations such as the NAACP have had to be watchful and intercede to see that children get what they deserve.

I sometimes visit schools where there are very few African American children, maybe seven or eight in a student population of two hundred or more. In some schools, these children are confident, greeting me, along with the other children, as I pass them in the corridors. Even those who appear shy will look at me and smile. But in other schools, the children refuse to look at me. They turn their eyes away, asking me silently not to do anything that would remind their white friends that they are not white. In these cases, I know that the children are not being allowed to feel comfortable with themselves and their African heritage.

Once I heard a small group of African American girls talking about beauty. They said that although they knew they weren't beautiful on the outside, they were beautiful inside. Physical beauty is not, of course, nearly as important as inner beauty. But as I watched the girls, I was saddened because they had no idea how beautiful they were. I wondered what they saw when they looked in the mirror.

I have met other children who feel the same way about themselves. They have been taught, partly by society at large, but also by the attitudes of some adults and children in their schools, to believe the myth that one kind of beauty is superior to others.

Many of the schools I visit are working to resolve problems such as these. They understand that there is a benefit for all children when they can meet and respect each other. All of them have something to give that can enrich the lives of others.

Racism, no matter what the circumstances, is difficult and dangerous. In some ways, the Supreme Court decision of 1954 exchanged one set of problems for another. But the decision was important and necessary. No door should be closed to any of America's citizens. All Americans must be able to walk freely in the country they and their ancestors have helped to build.

This legacy, then, is a precious gift of courage, dedication, and struggle. An inheritance handed by each generation to the next, it is seen in the lives of teachers who teach and children who learn, in spite of the odds against them. But the story is bigger than that. It encompasses people in every field doing what they do, in the best way they can, to make life better for the generations of children to come.

ELOISE GREENFIELD is the celebrated poet and author of more than forty books for children. Her many awards include the Coretta Scott King Medal and two Coretta Scott King Honors.

ANTHONY

by Lois Lowry

"**H**E'S CRYING. We were playing keepaway, and he just started to cry." My children, all four of them, came thundering through the back door into the kitchen, where I was stirring spaghetti sauce. "What should we do?"

I glanced out the window of the Maine farmhouse and saw him standing in the backyard. Sneakers untied. Head down. Skinny shoulders heaving. Tasha, our Newfoundland dog, was at his side, loving but unhelpful. Quickly, I wiped my hands on a paper towel and headed out to try to comfort him. "You guys stay inside," I said. "Set the table. Seven places, remember, not six."

"Let's fold his napkin funny," I heard one of them say to the others. "It'll make him laugh."

Anthony had arrived that afternoon. He was six years old and had just finished first grade. He had ridden that day seven hours in a bus from New York City. Now he was in our backyard in Maine waiting to have dinner with six blue-eyed, blond people whom he had never met before in his life. I didn't blame him for crying.

I had not specified age, gender, or race when I applied to take a Fresh Air Child into my home that summer of 1968. My own four children were two boys and two girls, and they ranged in age from six to ten. Whoever arrived on that bus would find a niche somewhere in our family. There were plenty of toys to share, an assortment of bathing suits for borrowing, and room for one more at the table. The dog adored children indiscriminately, and the cat ignored everyone with the same amount of disdain.

But when they called my name at the Greyhound station, and a little African American boy, wide-eyed, wearing a name tag with ANTHONY on it, appeared at the door of the bus, I found myself thinking: *He's so small.*

My own son, Ben, was also six and had also just completed first grade. But watching the two boys as they walked side by side to the station wagon (Anthony lugging his small plastic suitcase, refusing any help), I could see that Ben was a head taller.

"Shall we call you Tony?" I asked him as the children arranged themselves in the back of the car.

He glared at me. "Why?"

"Well, ah, I meant that Tony is a nickname for Anthony. So maybe you like to be called Tony?"

"No."

My son came to my rescue. "My name's Benjamin, but I like to be called Ben. Look, I can touch the ceiling of the car with my feet."

"So can I." These were pre-seat-belt days. Anthony lay on the seat of the car beside Ben and they touched the dome light with their sneakers. In the rearview mirror I watched the skinny legs, white and brown, vie for positioning.

His brief tears in the yard before supper came simply from a lot of fatigue, a little homesickness, and a certain amount of uncertainty about spaghetti, which he claimed never to have tasted before. But dinner was a hit. Slurping spaghetti was fun. He laughed in the bathtub, and made a soapsud beard, copying Ben. The two little boys traded pajamas; Anthony wore Ben's baseball players in return for the Tarzans folded in Anthony's little suitcase.

They were ironed. "Your mom *irons* your pajamas?" I asked him in astonishment. His answering look said, *You mean you don't?* I let it pass.

As night fell, all five of them, smelling of shampoo, arranged themselves on the yellow couch where we gathered every evening, and I opened a book to read aloud as I always did.

The reading ritual was new to Anthony.

"Doesn't your mom ever read to you?" one of the kids asked him.

"She too *busy*," he replied defensively. (Ironing pajamas? I wondered.)

Over the summer we would learn more about Anthony's superindustrious mom. She was a lawyer, a doctor. Rock star. Bank president. She rode a Harley, sang with the Beatles, had been in the paratroops, spoke several languages. Hardly a moment to read stories at bedtime.

"Well, what about your teacher at school? Doesn't she read stories to the class?" I asked him.

Anthony grinned. "She yell at us, is all." He

snuggled in and watched the pages. "What it say there? Don't turn so fast."

"That's just the title page," I told him. "The story doesn't begin yet."

"Read it," Anthony commanded. So I back-tracked and read the title page to him. The book was by an author named Dayton Hyde, I told him.

"He the guy wrote it down?"

"Yes. Dayton Hyde is his name. And the title of the book he wrote is—"

Ben interrupted. Ben was proud of having learned to read this year. "*Cranes in My Corral,*" he read, with his finger following the words on the title page.

Anthony pushed Ben's finger away. "He get that right?" he asked me. "Is that what it say?"

"Yes. That's the title. *Cranes in My Corral.*"

"Lemme see where it say that."

I showed him the words of the title and he repeated it. I could see that it was going to be a long evening.

It was our custom to read one chapter of a book each night at bedtime. Dayton Hyde's book (now sadly out of print) was a charming true story of a family of sandhill cranes that nested on his ranch, disappeared each year as part of their migration, and returned faithfully every spring. By the end of the first chapter, the cranes had acquired personalities, and of course the star was the goofy, mischievous littlest one.

Anthony looked startled when I closed the book at the end of chapter one.

"Finish it," he demanded.

But finally he reluctantly accepted the fact that it was bedtime and that the story would resume the next night. With the too-long legs of Ben's baseball pajamas dragging on the floor, he climbed the stairs to bed.

He was an intelligent, curious, energetic, and very determined child. When, the next day, the application for the usual summer swimming lessons arrived and stipulated that each child must be at least four feet in height, I measured Anthony and found that he was simply not tall enough. But he glowered when I explained to him that he wouldn't be able to go.

"We'll find something fun to do while they go to swimming lessons," I told him, but he ignored me and disappeared, scowling, into the bathroom.

When he emerged, he ordered me to measure

him again. He had stuffed folded washcloths into his sneakers, elevating his feet uncomfortably at least an inch, and he had raked his hair up with a comb, trying to make it stand in the air.

It didn't make him four feet tall, but it made me go to the phone and wheedle a dispensation for this one too-small child so that he could learn to swim.

On his third morning in our home, I asked him if he would like to send a postcard to his mother to tell her that he had arrived safely and settled in.

He shrugged and said no.

"Well, you could tell your brothers and sisters that we have a horse and a dog and a cat."

The prospect of such gloating seemed to appeal to him, but he still said no.

"You write it," he said. "I be telling you what to say."

So I wrote the postcard message that he dictated, telling his family that he could not only swim but do award-winning dives, and that he knew how to cook spaghetti. I addressed it to the Bronx housing project address that I'd been given, and handed him the card so that he could sign his name.

He didn't know how. I held my hand over his

on the pen, and we made the letters together: ANTHONY. I showed him his name tag, which we had hung on the kitchen bulletin board, and he looked at it with some interest, now that he knew the name was his. Then he took his card to the mailbox, and lifted the small tin flag to let the rural mailman know that ANTHONY had written to his mother, who was herself, he told us, a mailman on the days when she wasn't being a violin player or a chef.

Each evening he was first on the couch, with the book in his hands. I showed him how the word *crane* looked on the page, and that he could, if he tried, find it in other places. From time to time his small index finger crept onto the page, to point to another sighting of the word as I read.

I don't remember how many chapters *Cranes in My Corral* contains. But I remember clearly the night that we read the final one.

Summer was passing. Anthony had learned to dog-paddle his way across the pool. He had sat on our horse and had had his picture taken, and the photograph was inside his suitcase waiting to be shown to his pals and siblings in New York. He had eaten lobster, and then he had eaten more lobster, and still more. He was hoping to eat twelve lobsters by the time he went home. Next summer, he said, he would come back and eat *forty* lobsters, and he would not only sit on the horse next summer, but he would let the horse *walk* while he was sitting.

I read the last chapter of the book. One more time, the family of cranes returns to Mr. Hyde's ranch corral. One by one they appear in the distance, and then swoop in to their familiar place, the place where they had been born and to which they had been returning for years. The rancher waits and watches. But one crane—the littlest one, the one we all liked best, the goofy, silly one—is missing. Hours pass, and finally night comes. But the last crane has, on its travels, met with some mishap. It does not return.

I closed the book. My own children nodded their heads, accustomed to endings, accepting of sadness. They began to gather themselves to head upstairs to bed.

But Anthony sat stunned. "What happened next?" he asked me. "Read me the next."

"That's the end, Anthony. See? No more chapters." I showed him the book, how the page I had just read was the last page.

He flipped the end pages, looked at the back flap, inside the back cover, searching hopelessly for more story.

"Come on, Anth," Ben said. "We can play army men in our room before we go to bed."

But Anthony was crying. He held the book in his arms. "I wanted *more!*" he wailed.

When we took Anthony to the bus station for his trip back to New York, he greeted his fellow travelers, each of them name-tagged once more, some of them sunburned, one with an arm in a cast, all of them weighted with souvenirs. Anthony carried a shopping bag filled with seashells, two empty lobster claws, a snorkeling mask, and our copy of *Cranes in My Corral*.

He returned the following summer: seven years old now, a seasoned traveler with a list of expectations that included a stop at Weeks' Ice Cream en route home from the bus station.

He had finished second grade. He looked at the menu in the ice-cream shop and grinned at the familiar garish photos of sundaes. "Can you read it?" I asked, pointing to a description of his favorite.

"Not yet," he replied. "But I'll learn."

Nor could he read at eight, the third summer he spent with us, after he had completed third grade.

Ben was also eight, that summer, and my other children were nine, eleven, and twelve. My oldest, a girl now in junior high, wanted to watch the evening news to see what was happening in Vietnam, and her one-year-younger brother had ball games to play, games that lasted into the summer twilights. They no longer joined us on the yellow couch each evening. Now it was only Ben, Kristin, Anthony, and me.

"He can't read a single word, Mom," Ben confided privately. "Not even *Green Eggs and Ham*. And he's going into fourth grade!"

I knew that. And it troubled me. But when I tried to show Anthony the sounds of letters, the magic of their combinations, he became impatient. "My teacher will teach me that," he insisted. "I'll learn when school starts." He didn't want school, not in summer. He wanted stories.

Night after night, for three summers, we sat on that yellow couch, Tasha the Newfoundland snoring at our feet, and journeyed through books. The cool barn where Charlotte lived and died, the primordial swamp where dinosaurs roamed, space and rocket ships, Oz and Narnia: all of them became the landscape of Anthony's life in our family. Each August he went home with books in his suitcase, stories in his heart, and the expectation that this year would be the year when he would learn to read.

His confidence and resilience astounded me. In Maine, I had watched him jump into water well over his head and seen him bob back up grinning and make his way back to the dock with a city-boy dog paddle that somehow kept him afloat. I had seen him fall from a horse and feed the horse a forgiving apple from our orchard. He had ridden a chairlift, brown legs dangling, to the top of a ski slope, then hiked back down and found the untied sneaker that had dropped from his foot midway. It had never occurred to him that the water was too deep or too cold, that the horse's big teeth might bite too far, or that the sneaker would not be right there at the base of the tall pine.

And each September he embarked happily on another year in school, certain that he would catch on this time, would break the code, would become a reader. "This year I will," he said with determination each fall.

And each year it didn't happen.

The spring that Ben, now nine, finished fourth grade, I sent in our annual application for Anthony's visit. By this time it was routine. But this time there was no reply.

I called the organization that sponsored the visits and they checked their records. Anthony's mother had not sent in the paperwork this year, they told me.

Perhaps she was ill? Surely not; not Anthony's mother, who was herself a doctor as well as a nurse, and a veterinarian and professional wrestler to boot? I asked them to call her with a reminder, to tell her we were looking forward to our fourth summer with her son.

They tried. But the telephone was disconnected. There was no one by that name at the address.

And so that optimistic, valiant little boy disappeared from our lives. We never saw Anthony, never heard from him again.

What does any of this have to do with *Brown v. Board of Education*, that decision handed down fourteen years before a child named Anthony entered my kitchen carrying a little plastic suitcase?

I'm not at all sure. Sadly, it's a reminder that the

Supreme Court of the United States could not decree an end to every problem that an African American child, heart filled with hope, would face in today's world. The court couldn't mandate caring classrooms or fine teachers with a reverence for literacy. But it gave children like Anthony the right to expect those things, to hope for them, to demand them.

My son Ben is a lawyer now, and has two little boys of his own. Every night they curl up beside him, wearing Spider-Man pajamas, and listen to the stories he reads.

From time to time I think about Anthony, and wonder where he is. Statistics tell me that a little black boy growing up thirty years ago in a Bronx project had a pretty good chance of becoming a dropout, a drug addict, a criminal, or a corpse. But I don't think those things happened to Anthony.

I think that in his case, the statistics were offset by other things: that he had a mother who was right up there with Wonder Woman—and who ironed his pajamas; that at six years old, not yet four feet tall, he had carried his own suitcase into the home of strangers and made himself a place; that he

cherished books and was determined to master reading no matter how long it took.

I think that today—tonight, this very night—
somewhere he is holding his own child on his lap,
and reading a story aloud.

LOIS LOWRY is the author of several beloved books for
children and has received many awards, including two
Newbery Medals for *The Giver* and *Number the Stars*.

ST. LOUIS

by Quincy Troupe

THE 1950s were a terrible time for blacks and other people of color living in the United States. All kinds of injustices were rampant, including blatant bias and discrimination in employment, housing, use of public facilities, sports, entertainment and publishing, education, and the enforcement of laws. In fact, officially authorized police brutality, murder, and lynching of innocent people of color, but especially black males, were the order of the day.

During the summer of 1955, I saw the horrible photographs in *Jet* magazine of Emmett Till—the fourteen-year-old black male teenager who was lynched in Mississippi—and his bloated, mutilated body that was dropped into the Tallahatchie River. Emmett Till was from Chicago and was unaware of the racist "Southern customs" common in Mississippi and throughout the South. Supposedly, he had said "Bye, baby," to a white woman in a grocery store. For this transgression he was dragged from his bed in the middle of the night, kidnapped, beaten to a pulp, and his testicles were cut off; and then he was shot dead on the spot, which probably mercifully ended his excruciatingly painful and horrible suffering. The "good ol' white boys" who killed him also tied a very large weight around his neck and dumped his violated young body into the Tallahatchie River. After these men, grinning from ear to ear, were caught and jailed, a local white jury acquitted them and let them go free, despite the fact that they had both confessed to the crime.

The behavior of these white men and their unpunished crime were typical of the racial climate in which I and many other blacks lived prior to the civil rights movement of the 1960s.

It is fair to say that the 1950s were characterized by an absolute arrogance among most white people. It was a period accompanied by an almost complete indifference to the needs and suffering of blacks and other nonwhites. A common attitude among whites in the United States, which was no different in St. Louis, Missouri, where I was born and raised, was an almost imperial sense of self-righteousness, an absolute conviction that black people (and indeed all people of color) were inferior in all things, except sloth, criminal intent, and ignorance.

I don't remember any white people in St. Louis speaking out against Emmett Till's brutal lynching. Nor do I recall anyone white seeming to even care about the senseless injustice of his murder. For me, there had to be something terribly wrong with the basic, so-called Christian morality of this country, when racist outrages like the murder of Emmett Till (and many other blacks) could occur right under their noses. But this never seemed to cross the minds of the few whites with whom I came into contact.

Looking back, it seems to me that most whites thought it wasn't up to them as individuals or as a group to do anything about the situation. They seemed to feel that the burden of solving the race problem in this country lay solely on the shoulders of black people. As a matter of fact, most whites seemed to think the best solution for them was to look the other way and to ignore the predicament of blacks in this country. The great majority of them did just that, too, and their attitude only helped to worsen the problem.

In truth, American whites weren't the only ones guilty of burying their heads in the sand during this shameful period of our history. Many African Americans also played a key role in their own undoing by "going along to get along" and not raising their voices in unified protests against the horrible injustices inflicted on all black people in this country and abroad. Many of these duplicitous blacks just out-and-out "Tommed" for the white power structure. That is, for their own personal financial gain, many blacks acted as spies for whites, because, often, many blacks—because of the atrocities inflicted on them since the days of slavery — believed in their own inferiority.

Yet, although the 1950s were a dark time for African Americans, the 1954 *Brown v. Board of Education* decision dangled before blacks the tantalizing promise of greater access to success and riches through integration and equal access to public education. This was the expectation that my mother and my stepfather, China Brown, had when they moved our family (my brother Timmy and me; my mother's mother, Leona Smith; and Leona's son Allen). We moved from Delmar and Leonard in an all-black neighborhood in downtown St. Louis to Ashland, an all-white, lower middle-class neighborhood in North St. Louis, during the summer of 1955. Except for our family and an elderly black couple who lived next door to us, there were no other blacks in our neighborhood.

My mother had moved us to within one and a half blocks of Beaumont High School, a previously all-white school. She believed that by sending me to an all-white school she was making it possible for me to have a better education and a better life. But, in reality, in 1955 at age sixteen, I didn't want to leave my friends at Vashon High School and transfer to a new school, because I had known some of my friends since the third grade. I didn't know how I was going to make new friends at a new school, especially since I knew there would be so few students like me there. Even though we lived only one and a half blocks from Beaumont High School, the walk to school seemed to take forever, because I dreaded what would happen to me in my classroom, in the hallways, and on the playgrounds.

When I first transferred to Beaumont High, I

was among the first group of black students to attend the school. I was one of seven blacks students in a sea of three thousand mostly hostile white students. At Beaumont we were physically and verbally threatened, ambushed, beaten, and chased down the halls. One time, a gang of white boys threw black ink on one of our classmates, Claudia Tibbs, who was a very light-skinned, very beautiful girl, and told her to "turn back to her natural color." I didn't like being around so many students who so obviously hated me, and they didn't want to be around me either. They had been taught to believe the same things their parents believed, that black people were inferior to them.

I didn't want to go out for the basketball team because of this hostility. Eventually, I did, and I helped the school win a state basketball championship. I didn't want to raise my hand in class because I was afraid the teachers would make fun of the way I talked, which they did. I remember one time I raised my hand to answer a question in my history class. Even though I gave the correct answer to the teacher, she made fun of the way I spoke. She pretended not to understand what I had said, and she asked me in a very nasty tone of voice, "Where'd you learn how to talk like that? Didn't your mother ever teach you to speak proper English?" The entire class broke into loud and long laughter, and I was very embarrassed, angry, and upset, but there was nothing I could do but sit there and be ridiculed. I decided that I would never again raise my hand in that class, and despite her many efforts to get me to participate in her class after that, I always refused. During this time, hardly any of my teachers or the school principal ever protected me from the abuse the other black students and I suffered at the hands of the white students. In fact, it was the vice principal of the school who got angry with me and reprimanded me when I danced with a white female student at one of the school dances. I didn't think that I would ever feel at home at this school or ever be close to any of the whites who attended it.

Just as I disliked leaving all my friends at Vashon, I was also unhappy to move into a new neighborhood so far away from them. Even though we lived in a nicer house and in a "better" neighborhood—in a home with a backyard that was on a street shaded by oak and elm trees—I missed my friends from the old neighborhood very much. However, my loneliness would be short-lived because, soon enough, our white neighbors all moved away, as other black families moved in.

In the long run, though, the *Brown* decision did change things in a very fundamental way for blacks and whites alike. We were integrated. Integration brought us in contact with each other in ways we had not been allowed in the past. Now we were able to sit side by side in the same classroom, in movie theaters, and on buses. With integration, we ate side by side in the same restaurants and used the same public toilets. Now we sat side by side on the same benches in the park, swam in the same public swimming pools in summer, lived in the same neighborhoods, and competed for the same jobs.

By making it possible for me to attend school with whites, the *Brown* decision helped to demystify the power whites had previously held over me. They no longer seemed invincible, because now I could see up close their weaknesses, as well as their strengths. And I realized right away that I could compete with and often surpass whites in the class-room, in sports, in everything, just as I had sur-passed other students at Vashon High School. So in this sense, integration was beneficial for me, even though almost every white person I knew in Beaumont High School—with the exception of Tom Palazzola, an Italian teenager I met on the basketball team—shunned me and rarely had a friendly word for me (not to mention never socializing with me, or any of the other black kids, for that matter). For most of the white students at Beaumont High, we blacks were like lepers. Yet nothing changed at Beaumont until the blacks started to fight back. And fight back hard some of us did, with determination, resolution, and sometimes, with our fists. My life changed forever when I realized that, even though we were integrated, blacks in the United States would never get anything we needed unless we fought for it.

At the same time, the *Brown* decision had not only a tremendous and lasting impact on education but over time, a far-reaching and paradoxically debilitating effect on black businesses and other institutions as well. With integration, black sports leagues (such as the Negro Baseball Leagues) and some other all-black cultural, religious, and enter-tainment institutions disappeared. Many black busi-nesses, banks, and credit unions, which had grown deep roots in black communities across the country, gradually closed as their customers scattered among

newly integrated urban and suburban neighborhoods. Many black communities and businesses lost
the bulk of their best and most educated minds to
white suburbs and white corporations. What little
economic control African Americans had over their
lives eroded significantly.

I have witnessed the collapse of many solidly
middle-class black neighborhoods all over St. Louis
since the *Brown* decision. And as they imploded following the loss of jobs and patronage, they took
down with them many venerable cultural, religious,
and financial institutions. The *Brown* decision
inadvertently contributed to transforming black
communities into urban ghettos all over the United
States.

And have the schools in St. Louis and other
urban areas been integrated since *Brown v. Board of
Education*? It seems it takes more than fifty years to
change a system and a way of thinking that has been
in place for generations. Today there is a growing
resegregation of America's schools and the concen-
trated poverty of students in largely black schools
places the future of millions of black children at
risk. The average family income of a black child
today is far lower than that of whites, and family

income is closely related to educational levels. At the same time, the rapid growth of the black middle class is a direct result of the increasing number who hold college degrees; and the children whose parents attended college are highly likely to follow them into higher education.

There is no doubt that even the children in black middle-class families suffer from the legacy of the Jim Crow schools in which their grandparents and earlier generation of blacks received inferior education. Blacks in this country have been struggling long and hard to get what we need. We've come a long way in fifty years, but we haven't come far enough.

QUINCY TROUPE is an award-winning poet, performer, producer, editor, and children's book author, whose books include *Take It to the Hoop, Magic Johnson*.

THE PROPHET

by Katherine Paterson

"THEY'RE HERE!"

Annoyed at being interrupted, I looked up to see an underclassman standing in my dorm door. She was obviously agitated.

"What do you mean?"

"The Supreme Court said we had to go to school with them, and they're already here!"

"Huh?" I was lost in the paper I was trying to write and had no idea what she was talking about.

"Come look out my windows if you don't believe me."

I went with her. A crowd of girls was huddled by the windows in the large corner room. From the side window you could see the road coming up the hill from the main gate of the campus. From the front you could see the green and the college buildings gathered around it. It was a brilliant spring afternoon, the kind that made you want to lie outside in the sun, not stay inside writing your final papers and studying for exams.

"See?" My attention was directed toward the side window. There they came, maybe as many as a dozen young men, laughing and joking with one another as they walked up the main road and turned onto the narrower pavement around the green. They all seemed very tall and very black.

"See? What did I tell you?"

"Well, they didn't waste any time, did they?" another of my friends said. "They only announced the decision this afternoon, and here they are already, coming to take over our campus."

"Oh, I don't think so," I remember saying, but my voice sounded puny even to me. The fear in the room was palpable and infectious. "I can't believe those guys are here to take over the school."

But what did I know? What did any of us white Southerners know that spring day how *Brown v. Board of Education* might shake our tranquil lives? Perhaps it was guilt, perhaps it was the unknown quality of the future that had been torn open that day, but most of us, even those of us whose minds told us not to be silly were apprehensive.

I was born in China, one of a handful of non-Chinese to live in our city of more than a million people. Our family lived in a Chinese house, and all our immediate neighbors, those who lived within the walls of our compound, were Chinese. If we went outside our gates we might hear ourselves called "foreign devils," but I never thought of myself as a foreigner inside those walls. I became a foreigner when war forced us to evacuate to the United States. We came first to Virginia and later moved to North Carolina, and there was much about this strange land that I could not understand.

I remember a peculiar conversation I had with a young woman who had been hired to help my mother. She was Negro (the word my parents insisted upon), as most Southern domestic help was in those days. I hate to think what her wages must have been.

"Where are you from?" I asked her.

She was working and not eager to talk to

me. "I'm from Richmond," she said.

"No, not now," I said. "I mean what's your real country? What language do you really speak?"

She looked at me as though I'd lost my mind. "I'm American," she said. "I speak English."

"You can't be," I insisted, my early experience having taught me that people with different-color skin lived in other countries and spoke other languages. She was treating me as though I was being rude, and I wasn't rude, I was interested. Why wouldn't she tell me the truth?

It wasn't long before white society set me straight. The Negroes I met did indeed belong in America, but, and no one quite put this into words, they belonged in a different way—that's why they went to different schools and different churches and lived in separate neighborhoods.

I had no playmates as a child who were Negro. In fact, Ruth and Asalee were the only Negroes I really knew. Even though, compared to our schoolmates and the people in the church where my father worked, we were poor, we had enough money to hire a maid. Ruth was the first person who worked for our family when we lived in Winston-Salem, North Carolina. It is significant that I have no last name for her even though she was a powerful personality in our lives. All five of us children were in awe of Ruth, who immediately mastered our mother's "come home" whistle. When Ruth whistled, we raced home. When she spoke, we listened. When she ordered, we jumped. She took us to programs at the Negro Teacher's College, where, as I recall, she was getting a degree while she worked for us. Anyhow, one day she left us to go on to better things. I've often thought that had she been born a few years later she might have been the first African American woman senator from North Carolina.

Ruth's successor was a teenager named Asalee. We liked Asalee, but we certainly didn't stand in awe of her, nor did we feel the need to obey her. That never seemed to bother Asalee, who was a free, if somewhat flighty, soul. It was wartime, and our mother went almost daily to meetings either at the church or the Red Cross. Once Mother was out of sight, Asalee would call a friend who owned a car and, with my two younger sisters in tow, take off for home. My younger sisters remember crouching hidden on the floorboards as they were driven out to the Negro section of town. I'm sure our mother never found out about these visits. She was genuinely fond of Asalee, but those clandestine car rides might have made her think twice about leaving her preschool daughters in Asalee's care.

We left Winston-Salem in 1946. Once again we lived in Richmond, but my parents could no longer afford domestic help. There was no Ruth or Asalee coming to our apartment. So, although we lived in a Southern city, segregated housing and segregated schools insured that that other half of the population was strangely invisible to us.

One incident stands out from those years. The Negro movie theater downtown was showing the film *Green Pastures,* and my father wanted to take us children to see it. He called the theater to see if it would be all right for us to come. Whoever he talked to was polite, but made it clear that white patrons were not welcomed. I had lived since I was eight and a half in a land of separate schools, separate churches, separate entrances, separate rest rooms, even separate drinking fountains, all of which I had come to accept as "the way things were." But now, at fourteen, when refused entrance to a Negro movie house, I felt a foreign sensation—guilt? regret? shame? I didn't even know how to name the feeling.

I'm sure reading this, you're appalled. How could the many African Americans in whose midst I lived be almost invisible to me? How could I be unaware of the pain and injustice that existed in the various cities and towns in which I lived, all of them cruelly divided by race? I was not totally lacking in sensitivity. I certainly knew when teachers or peers regarded me as inferior or treated me as though I were invisible. I knew when classmates suffered injustice, even when I was too cowardly to act on their behalf. Why did this sensitivity stop at the color line? It was not until I was seventeen that a book began to pry open my eyes. It was the summer of 1950. I was working at a Presbyterian conference center in the mountains of North Carolina, and my roommate was a missionary kid, raised in the Belgian Congo. Mary read aloud Alan Paton's remarkable novel about South Africa, *Cry, the Beloved Country*. The African names, places, and expressions that would have hindered the flow of the story for me rolled mellifluously off her tongue. It was the beauty of the language that enchanted me, and then the horror of the story. For the first time in my life I began to see the "way things were." Alan Paton's devastating story of South Africa became a story of my tragically divided South—the injustice and killing prejudices of the white minority of his country became the sins of my people, my country, my sins.

It was the following summer that I made my first African American friend. I had just finished my freshman year in college, and she was a teacher in a segregated high school. Why Verna honored me with her friendship, I do not know. I was in no way her peer, intellectually or spiritually, but she treated me as though I were. I think she could accept me the way I was and love me because she had fully accepted and loved herself. She talked frankly and openly about the way things were and the way they ought to be. Knowing her forced me to grow, but I never felt forced, only nourished.

Though my summers were times of growth, I went back to my segregated life when fall came. The only African Americans on our college campus worked in the service areas. And so when those young black men came up the hill on the day *Brown v. Board of Education* was hailed with joy and hope on the other side of town, it was greeted with fear on ours. Even I, who knew better, who argued with my friends that the appearance of those young men was not a hostile takeover, shared their fear of the unknown. Retribution was long overdue, and who could imagine what form it might take. The *Brown* Decision in 1954 did not result in immediate desegration of schools. There was tremendous resistance in many states; change was slow.

The following year, I taught in a still segregated elementary school, and then I went on to the Presbyterian School of Christian Education in Richmond, Virginia, where I had lived twice before. For the first time I sat in class and lived in a dorm with an African American student. We only had one, but Betty Jean was a beginning. In the middle of the year, I skipped school to take a Greyhound back to Winchester, Virginia, where my parents lived. I felt I had to go home to vote against a proposed amendment to the Virginia state constitution which would have closed the public schools rather than desegregate them—not exactly a world-shaking act on my part, but a baby step in the right direction.

The summer of 1956 I was working in a church in Nashville, Tennessee. One afternoon I got a phone call from a friend. "I want you to come with me to Fisk tonight," she said. "There's a young man speaking at the college who is going to be the next American prophet."

As I remember it, Peg and I were the only two white people in the audience, but we were all electrified by the speaker. "Only love," he told us, "is powerful enough to conquer evil." The young prophet was Martin Luther King, Jr. He was twenty-six years old, I was twenty-three, and the Birmingham bus boycott had been going on for seven months.

I never took part in a sit-in, marched in a voting-rights protest, or rode a Freedom bus. I spent the years from 1957 to 1961 in Japan, and when I returned to the United States, the movement had left me far behind. My husband marched with African Americans seeking to register to vote in Greensboro, Alabama, and spent three days in the Selma jail. I stayed home with the children. So my progress to and from that day in 1954 when *Brown* was decided has been a curving, rocky road, rather than a straight and shining path.

Of course, there was a simple, nonrevolutionary explanation for those young men who came laughing

up the hill on May 17, 1954. The college board of
trustees was giving a formal dinner, and the young
men were the catering company's waitstaff. They had
been instructed to arrive at precisely five P.M. I have
often wished they could have known the stir they
caused in the women's dormitory that afternoon.
Wouldn't they have enjoyed it?

KATHERINE PATERSON is the author of numerous
award-winning books for children, including two Newbery
Medal winners, *Bridge to Terabithia* and *Jacob Have I Loved,* and
the Newbery Honor title *The Great Gilly Hopkins.*

STORMY WEATHER

by Joyce Carol Thomas

We're traveling from
Tracy, California, back to 1950s Ponca City
A town, etched in young memory
A segregated oasis
Where black teachers lesson us in the freedom
   of piano music
Mixing manners, and reading and
   arithmetic, and sacred sonnets
Oh, my Oklahoma
In our Studebaker we sweat through the heat
Of the Mojave Desert and lurch on into
   Texas

Mama is ill.
Her soft biscuit-brown arms have turned
   bony and pale

Dr. Sonnenberg has told her she can make
   the trip
As long as she takes her medication, with
   water
I am in charge of the doctor's instructions

"Sister, hand me my purse."
I am the older daughter and have the
   designated title of "Sister"
I watch to see that Mama takes her tablets on
   time
She swallows the pill, rinses it down with
   water

Hungry, we stop in Texas
"Y'all CAIN'T eat in here!" A gruff voice
   takes our money
Turns us away from his restaurant.
"Y'all go eat over yonder!"
He points to an outdoor picnic
   table,
Littered dirty with bird droppings, swarming
   with flies.
I cannot eat the sandwich or watermelon
My stomach jumps rope

On the Texas–Oklahoma border
We stop for gas
And water for Mama's medicine
"Sister, hand me my purse."
I pass the purse to Mama
She opens the bag and takes out her pill
She asks the attendant
"May I have a cup of water?"
"No," the man says, still counting our
    money.
Mama's face turns ashen
I look out the car window for a Sunday-
    school Jesus
Driving the money changers from the
    Temple
I pray for an everflowing stream
Or a cloudburst from a summer
    storm
Flooding a cup's worth of water
Enough for Mama to swallow her pill

I am "Sister"
But I cannot help her.
My mind screams at the attendant's
Face clouded by ignorance

His mannerless, mean-spirited
  arrogance
I want to smack the smirk from his lips

"Pray, Sister." Mama can read my angriest
  thoughts
I pray
A storm kicks up
Lightning flashes
A torrent of holy water
Baptizes our dusty car
Windshield wipers sing with laughter

"Sister, hand me my purse."
I leap from the car
And collect healing water
In the cup of watertight fingers
Mama sips raindrops
From my praying hands

At the station
The attendant gazes in disbelief
Struck dumber by this gift from God
As though he never knew the kindness of
  teachers and librarians

Or hugs from a mama with fluffy biscuit-
brown arms

I still pray
For stormy weather

JOYCE CAROL THOMAS received the National Book
Award for *Marked by Fire,* and a Coretta Scott King Award
honor for *Brown Honey in Broomwheat Tea.* She is the author of
many other celebrated books for children.

MIKE AND ME

by Michael Cart

"THERE IT IS," Mike announced, pulling his car to a stop at the curb and pointing to the imposing brick building on the corner.

It was a gray, bone-chilling cold winter's day in Topeka, and the trees in front of the two-story building were leafless skeletons. I shivered, and my friend Mike Printz turned up his car's heaters.

It was sometime in the early '90s, and I had come to Kansas from my sunny (and warm) home in southern California to visit this old friend, who had been the librarian at Topeka West High School for so many years.

A born educator, Mike managed to wait a whole hour after my arrival before briskly announcing that it was time for show-and-tell, for what he called "the two-dollar tour" of his hometown. A dozen years have passed since then and my memory isn't what it used to be, but I think that Mike, at this point, actually rubbed his hands together in anticipation.

I wasn't especially anxious to tour Topeka, but I knew there was no point in arguing with a man as stubborn as I am, so into his car we clambered and off we drove.

Though he had been animated and talkative at first, Mike now sat behind the wheel in silence, staring thoughtfully at our destination, the first stop on his promised tour.

I stared, too, searching for clues to the building's identity. Finding none, I finally broke the silence. "You win," I said, throwing my hands up in mock defeat. "What is it?"

Mike smiled, secretly pleased, I think, to have stumped me.

"It's the Monroe Elementary School," he explained. And when I remained perplexed, he added, "You know, *Brown v. Board of Education*."

"Oh," I said, as sudden awareness flooded over me.

I should have known. After all, Mike had such a keen and enthusiastic appreciation of Kansas history that he could make friends like me, who hadn't grown up in the Sunflower state, feel positively deprived. So what else, I thought with a smile, would he have chosen as the first stop on our tour but a school that was both an historic Kansas landmark *and* an enduringly universal symbol?

Located at Fifteenth and Monroe streets in southeast Topeka, Monroe Elementary was built in 1926, and until the U.S. Supreme Court's landmark 1954 ruling in *Brown* it had been one of four segregated elementary schools attended by African American students in the Kansas state capital.

I think often about that winter's day and in my mind's eye I still see Mike and me, two middle-aged white men contemplating a building that was so much more than just bricks and mortar.

Perhaps it was being in the presence of such a powerful piece of our nation's history that set me to thinking about my own personal history.

I was born in 1941 and grew up in Logansport, Indiana, a small town on the banks of the Wabash River. Both my parents' families originally came to this country from Germany, bringing with them traditional values and religious beliefs that included tolerance and at least a tacit acceptance of the dignity and worth of every individual. Being good Lutherans, though, we were also a tad suspicious of all those who weren't Lutherans, especially if they happened to belong to the Knights of Columbus or the local Masonic Lodge!

Be that as it may, I think we—and most of the people who lived in my hometown—were generally free of the more narrow-minded prejudices that infested so many small towns in the America of the 1940s and '50s and that, twenty years earlier, had made the Ku Klux Klan a political power in Indiana.

By the time I came along, who I was in my Hoosier hometown was not defined by race but by neighborhood, economic status, and church affiliation. I was a kid who lived on the north side of town, one of four homogeneous neighborhoods.

I was not a rich kid or a poor kid. I fit somewhere in the middle. Church was important because it offered the only opportunity I had to meet kids who lived in different parts of town. Until I went to high school, that is. Since there was only one high school, everybody wound up together in the same informal melting pot of a building.

Blacks, in the years before 1954, wound up in the same melting pot. For there was no official segregation in my hometown, and skin color was never much of a factor—not because we were especially enlightened, but because there were so few black people. In my high school class of 289 students, for example, only four were African American. And of the entire city-county population, less than one half of one percent was black.

Two of my very early, pre-1954 memories spring from my family's living in the South for a year when I was four.

We returned to the South periodically for visits. On one of those visits my mother held a door open for a black woman who seemed thunderstruck by what seemed to me to be no more than a routine act of human courtesy.

Was it possible, I wondered—without quite having the words to express the thought—that my mother had done something, well, *unusual* for that time and place?

More powerful, though, was my seeing a sign above a drinking fountain that said, simply, WHITES ONLY. I had heard of such things when I was around eight or nine years old, that in some parts of the country black people were not permitted to drink from the same fountains as whites or to use the same bathrooms. This, however, was my first personal encounter with this horrible reality.

I was puzzled. This was the first time I had seen something so far outside my normal experience that at first I couldn't quite figure out what it was that I was seeing. When comprehension finally came, I suddenly felt viscerally and deeply ashamed of being white. And I felt angry, too, at what I recognized as a horrible injustice.

As a boy I was no stranger to injustice. I was an anomaly, a boy who loved to read, a boy who hated sports in a small town that was crazy for baseball, football, basketball, a boy who was generally regarded as the smartest kid in class, a courteous, well-behaved teacher's pet. A sissy! And—perhaps worst of all—a boy who was fat.

I was a disappointment to my father, who had been a high-school football hero, and who longed for a son who was a *real* boy. I was the object of teasing, scorn, and ridicule on the playground. I despaired. I thought I would always be the butt of jokes.

Yes, I knew a lot about injustice. Yet, though it

was knowledge painfully learned, I am grateful, as an adult, for the experience because I recognize it helped me develop a social conscience and a deep-rooted empathy for all others who, for whatever reasons, were outsiders like myself.

I recognize that in those days I knew virtually nothing about the injustice that black people experienced so routinely and on such a daily basis.

I knew nothing about the reality of black life. For instead of real black people, all I had been exposed to were the stereotypical images of African Americans offered by the entertainment media. In my pre-television youth that meant seeing Buckwheat starring in *Little Rascal* film shorts. And it meant listening to the radio and laughing at characters like Amos and Andy and Beulah.

What did I think of my encounters with such stereotypical characters? Well, the truth is that I *didn't* think. These black people were presented as figures of fun, and in my innocence and ignorance, I focused on the jokes they made and that others made about them, not on the more important social implications of the experience.

Even worse, as an adult who has written a book about humor, I am ashamed to realize that I wasn't laughing *with* these characters, I was laughing *at* them. I was, in short, no better than the kids who laughed at me on the playground.

Fortunately, I had books to set the record straight, didn't I? Well, no I didn't. When I was young and anxious to read about the entirety of a world that extended beyond the city limits of Logansport, Indiana, one tremendously important segment of that larger world was almost entirely absent from books: the African American segment.

Two books by white authors Jerrold and Lorraine Beim did present a fairly authentic picture of black life. *Two Is a Team*, published in 1945, was one of the first stories of interracial friendship. *Swimming Hole*, published in 1950 when I was nine, was an early book about racial prejudice.

Though the Beims' stories seem simplistic today, they were, for their time, farsighted and powerful enough in dramatic terms that I still remember them fifty and more years later. They helped refine my thinking about injustice and the intrinsic value of every human being.

Nevertheless, the fact remains that these books, too, were written from *outside* the black experience. In this pre–*Brown v. Board of Education* world, only a mere handful of black writers enjoyed the opportunity to publish books written by them *within* the black experience.

It took the 1954 Supreme Court decision to begin to change this, to set the stage for what Professor Henrietta Smith calls the "literary explosion of works by African American authors and illustrators."

By that time, I had grown up, gone off to library school, and started my career as a librarian.

And so had my friend Mike, who was so proud of saying, "From us [librarians] young people learn to live with knowledge and care."

And he might have added, "with compassion." For in the wake of Mike's introduction to young Topeka students of the dire realities of apartheid, the members of the Topeka West Student Council voted to remove all the Coca-Cola machines from the school. Why? Because they had discovered that the company, at that time, still had ties to the South African apartheid government.

I think of these things as I remember the day that Mike gave me his two-dollar tour of Topeka and introduced me to the Monroe Elementary School.

As I look back over my *Booklist* magazine columns

of the past eight years, I realize that the chance for people of color to publish their own stories, "honestly and openly," as Jacqueline Woodson hoped, has finally arrived and, with it, a golden age of African American literature and a time of honest, open— and authentic—story sharing.

For this we can thank the authors themselves. We might also thank book-loving, book-promoting, student-respecting librarians.

Though Mike may be gone (he died in 1996), he is not forgotten. The Young Adult Library Services Association, in creating a new award in 1999 for the best young adult book of the year, named it the Michael L. Printz Award in his honor.

Best of all, in this present context, the winner of the first Printz Award, presented in the year 2000, was the distinguished black writer Walter Dean Myers.

Thinking of this, I imagine myself in a car again with my friend Mike, driving this time to Fresno. The Topeka road fades into the background, and then opens up to the highways of our American world.

On our trip we talk about books. I begin naming African American picture books, poetry collections, and young adult novels by the dozens. And this time, I'm the one rubbing my hands together in anticipation of our destination.

For when we reach Fresno State University, I am the tour guide, with my own show-and-tell surprise. We make our way to the Arne Nixon Center for the Study of Children's Literature.

There I show Mike the dozens of titles by African American authors now decorating the shelves of this wonderful repository of books for *all* young readers, regardless of skin color.

Our journey, which has taken us to little town libraries as well as big cities culminates in Mike's knowing that his years of promoting the publication of books by African American authors is now an ongoing reality. African Americans continue to delight us with stories, poems, and paintings. And their books refresh both thirsty young readers and us adults with their eloquence, authenticity, and art.

Mike would be so pleased.

MICHAEL CART is a nationally recognized expert in young adult literature and publishing and has long been active in the American Library Association. He is the author and editor of many books for children.

COLOR BLIND

by Ishmael Reed

I READ ABOUT the Supreme Court decision, which outlawed school segregation, on the way home from Buffalo Technical High school, where the student body was integrated.

I was not a good poster boy for integration. Having chosen the wrong school, I was failing some of my subjects. I had absolutely no aptitude for the shop and metallurgy classes that made up the core classes of the technical high school. My grades improved markedly when I transferred to an academic high school. There I met my Greek American friend Richard Mardirosian.

Before boarding the Michigan Avenue bus for

home, Richard and I would usually stop by an ice-cream parlor and discuss politics and current events with the Jewish owner. We'd trade jokes and clown around. (Richard showed artistic talent and went on to act in Hollywood movies.)

Little did I know that the *Brown* decision, which began the dismantling of segregation in schools and other areas of life, would end the black scene on Michigan Avenue where Richard and I learned about the decision from the newspaper headlines.

The decision would have an immediate effect on the black businesses and other institutions located in the area surrounding the ice-cream parlor. For example, the Vendome, a black-owned hotel where black baseball players of the segregated Negro leagues would stay, closed. Nearby were clubs, like the Club Moonglow, where top musicians played. On Club Moonglow's side was a huge mural depicting zoot suiters and chorus girls. A few blocks away was the black-owned Little Harlem Nightclub, which survived until it was destroyed by fire.

Born in the South, I was taken to Buffalo, New York, when I was four. In the South there was little for black kids to do. We weren't taken to museums or libraries. Older people entertained themselves with gossip and storytelling. With going to church, funerals, drinking moonshine, and playing checkers. When we went to the movies, it was a dress-up occasion.

I sold *The Afro-American* while living in the Buffalo projects. This black-owned Baltimore newspaper carried stories about lynchings and other atrocities against black people. My opinion of the South was that it was a pretty bad place.

In Buffalo, I knew very little about black history. I knew nothing of the struggles that blacks had waged against white supremacy since the first slavers arrived. I couldn't identify Ida B. Wells, William Wells Brown, Benjamin Mays, or W.E.B DuBois.

I hadn't heard of *Plessy v. Ferguson* (1896). *Plessy v. Ferguson* is a surreal document that refers to the white race as "dominant," yet gives more weight to the amount of "black blood" in one's veins than the amount of "white blood."

On June 7, 1892, Homer Plessy, the plaintiff, paid for first-class passage on the East Louisiana Railway. Homer Plessy was one-eighth black and seven-eighths white, but under Louisiana law, he was considered black. Plessy, however, because he was so light skinned, felt "entitled to every recognition, right, privilege, and immunity secured to the citizens of the United States of the white race by its Consitution and the laws. . . ." The railroad company "was incorporated by the laws of Louisiana as a common carrier and was not authorized to distinguish between citizens according to their race." Despite the railroad's policy, the police forcibly ejected Plessy from the "white" coach.

He was imprisoned, charged with "criminally [violating] an act of the general assembly of the state, approved July 10, 1890." The assembly had resolved that railroad cars be segregated. The majority of the Louisiana and U.S. Supreme courts decided against Plessy, the plaintiff. The Plessy decision set the precedent that "separate" facilities for blacks and whites were constitutional as long as they were equal. The "separate but equal" doctrine quickly extended to cover many areas of public life and would not be struck down until 1954 in the equally important *Brown v. Board of Education* decision, which explicitly overturned *Plessy*.

One example of how school segregation was used to justify segregation in travel was a precedent cited by the majority in the *Plessy v. Ferguson* case. The cited case was *Roberts v. City of Boston*, "in which the supreme judicial court of Massachusetts held that the general school committee of Boston had power to make provision for the instruction of colored children in separate schools established exclusively for them, and to prohibit their attendance upon the other schools."

Homer Plessy and the lone dissenting judge in his case, John Marshall Harlan, wouldn't be vindicated until civil rights legislation was passed during the 1960s, after black and white protesters challenged the Jim Crow laws in force since the post-Reconstruction era.

In his dissenting opinion, Justice Harlan pointed out that African Americans had risked their lives "for the preservation of the Union." He termed the majority decision "pernicious."

Plessy v. Ferguson, in establishing the separate-but-equal doctrine, was about accommodations. Both Frederick Douglass and Ida B. Wells protested the separate and inferior accommodations for African Americans. But the accommodations accorded African Americans were anything but equal. My mother, Thelma V. Reed, in her book, *Black Girl from*

Tannery Flats, writes about the segregated railroad cars in which blacks were forced to ride.

During the Jim Crow era, blacks always had to sit in the back of the bus, then the back of the streetcar, the back of the train, the back, back, back. But on coal-burning trains, blacks had to sit in the *front* of the train because the locomotive was connected to the front of the train. When the blacks would get off that train, they would be filthy with cinders and soot and ashes and debris all over their clothes and in their hair.

For the first six years of my education, I attended a school with an all-black student body in the ghetto. It was considered to be integrated, because the teachers were white. The teachers considered me a discipline problem. They accused me of acting "cute" and "smart." A black teacher named Hortense Butts, now Nash, however, gave me tickets to concerts and encouraged me. She was the only black teacher I had during my twelve-year education. But there were other, off-campus, teachers.

These off-campus teachers were our counselors and mentors in youth clubs at the black Michigan Avenue YMCA. After the nation moved toward integration, it was decided that there was no longer a need for a black YMCA. Many of our mentors and counselors, being middle class, moved to the suburbs.

Integration sent these off-campus teachers into the outer regions of the city, far away from our neighborhoods. One of the results of integration is our current hip-hop generation. Phyllis Chesler calls such youths "father-wounded." These youths accuse my generation of deserting them. Though there are many intellectuals and professionals who have remained behind and provided services to the black "inner city," many role models have vanished. Dr. Lawson Bush, author of *Can Black Mothers Raise Our Sons?*, told a group of health-care workers in Berkeley on June 28, 2002, that because it destroyed "the black community, desegregation is one the worst things that could have happened to blacks." Many would agree.

Yet given the experience of my mother's generation, it is obvious that segregation had an ugly side as well. It was psychologically oppressive and often led to brutal acts against African Americans. Under it, African Americans were at the mercy of the "dominant race," whose members could do with blacks what they felt like, with a wink and a nod from the kind of justice system that made it possible for Homer Plessy to lose in court.

Still, Dr. Lawson Bush has a point. The hip-hop generation will never know famous black zones like Twelfth Street and Vine in Kansas City, now silent. The ghetto areas that remain rarely have attractive parks, well-stocked libraries, and accessible health-care facilities. Most of what remains of these once strong "black cities" one can only experience through film and recordings in museums located there. Nor will today's young people know the other "black cities" that formed a nation within a nation. Most of them have been bulldozed over in the name of "urban renewal," which was, in actuality, black removal.

Integration also led to the admission of blacks into white colleges and universities, with an adverse effect on historically black colleges and universities, which had trained thousands of black professionals, artists, and leaders. While many black students had been taught by black teachers under segregation, they were now exposed to white teachers whose backgrounds left them ill equipped to relate to students from different racial backgrounds. This problem still exists. Only sixteen percent of the nation's public school teachers are members of minorities. On the college and university level the percentage is much lower.

In 1992, Supreme Court Judge Clarence Thomas wrote a separate opinion in *United States v. Fordice*, to express his view that maintaining "historically black institutions" should not be ruled unlawful. "It never ceases to amaze me," he said, "that the courts are so willing to assume that anything that is predominantly black must be inferior."

Though thousands of black students were sent to study in white schools, they lost the kind of support, understanding, and counseling made available to them by black teachers. Much of this came about as a result of the *Brown* decision. And although black parents and children both say they want education and school credentials in order to get a good job with good pay, even young black children quickly realize they need to develop survival strategies in school. Negative stereotypes about black intelligence, sometimes perpetuated by teachers in white schools, depresses test performance on everything from IQ tests to SATs.

The Supreme Court ruled in favor of the Reverend

Oliver Brown and his daughter, Linda. On May 17, 1954, Chief Justice Earl Warren read the unanimous decision of the court: "Does segregation of children in public schools solely on the basis of race, even though the physical facilities and other 'tangible' factors may be equal, deprive the children of the minority group of equal educational opportunities? We believe that it does. . . . We conclude that in the field of education the doctrine of 'separate but equal' has no place."

Was the campaign toward integration the right move? Yes and no.

Yes, because it gave the lie to white supremacy. When I began my schooling at an integrated school, I discovered that whites were not gods, but flesh and blood like the rest of us. There was the same range in the abilities of whites and blacks—from poor to mediocre to excellent.

Integration also meant less humiliation for those belonging to Dr. Martin Luther King, Jr.'s class. As long as they could pay, African Americans couldn't be denied the accommodations that were off-limits to them in the old days. It is said that President Lyndon Johnson became a convert to civil rights after he asked his black valet to escort his beagles to Texas. The valet said that he had trouble enough driving himself to Texas without taking some dogs along. He then lectured the president about the hardships encountered by blacks when they tried to travel interstate by automobile.

In the wake of *Brown* and the assassination of President Kennedy came the Civil Rights Act of 1964 and the Voting Rights Act of 1965, which led to the election of thousands of black officeholders in the South.

Though integration has been a mixed blessing, the advantages, I believe, outweigh the disadvantages. The process challenges the nation to live up to its ideals, and demonstrates that resistance to change can be stiff and in some cases unyielding. Some studies indicate that the nation is undergoing *reseg-regation* (as if full integration had been accomplished!). Many of the most stubborn in their resistance to integration and diversity are American whites, including some of our nation's leading white intellectuals. Though some black intellectuals, termed "black rejectionists" by Professor Martin Kilson, attempt to dismiss white flight and other forms of white resistance, such as enrolling white students in private schools, as the result of black "underclass" behavior in the "inner" cities, one notes that these whites also seem to have a difficult time getting along with those whom they designate as the model minorities.

Integration has been a challenge to all groups. But it has challenged whites the most, many of whom find it impossible to give up their white-skin privileges, their own inherited affirmative action.

What Justice Harlan argued in *Plessy* can also apply to *Brown*: "In the view of the constitution, in the eyes of the law, there is in this country no superior, dominant, ruling class of citizens. There is no caste here. Our constitution is color-blind and neither knows nor tolerates classes among citizens. In respect to civil rights, all citizens are equal before the law. The humblest is the peer of the most powerful. The law regards man as man, and takes no account of his surroundings or of his color when his civil rights as guaranteed by the supreme law of the land are involved."

ISHMAEL REED is a poet, musician, television producer, and playwright. He has taught at Harvard, Yale, and Dartmouth, and has twice been nominated for the National Book Award.

THE AWAKENING

by Jean Craighead George

THE SUNLIGHT was glistening on
the long needles of the loblolly pines as the school
librarian drove me through North Carolina's coastal
forest. We were on our way to her hometown, where
I was scheduled to speak to the children. I cannot
remember the librarian's name—it is lost in the haze
of fifty years gone by—but I do remember that she
was slender and wore her blond hair in a braid
around her head. At the end of our brief introduc-
tions she told me her joy in life was opening the door
of her library each morning and helping a child find
just the right book to read. Then she added, "Maybe
someday I'll help Negro children, too. I pray for that

time to come." In those days we called African Americans or blacks "Negroes." Music was playing softly on the car radio. The day was May 17, 1954.

For the next ten minutes or so as we drove through primeval forest we chatted about schedules, restaurants, and special books. When the small talk ended we rode in thoughtful silence. Presently the librarian spoke.

"How do you feel about *Brown v. Board of Education*?" This was not an unusual question at that time, as the U.S. Supreme Court had been debating this case for two years and the nation was keenly interested.

"We must—and are going to—desegregate schools," I said, "but I don't think it will happen soon. The Supreme Court judges have been going back and forth for almost a year as to whether or not it should be done at all, and if it is, how quickly—a month, a year, two years. How quickly do you think it should happen?"

"Immediately," the librarian answered forthrightly. "Judge Thurgood Marshall has proved that segregated schools are 'separate but *not* equal,' and that 'separate but not equal schools' have a seriously detrimental effect on Negro children. They feel inferior. A sense of inferiority blocks the motivation to learn. It's time to right a terrible wrong."

I looked out the window. A woodpecker flew across the road, dipping and flicking in the manner of woodpeckers. I usually make a note of birds I see in the different states I visit, but not this time. I did not even note his species. I was thinking about third grader Linda Brown in Topeka, Kansas, walking a mile through a railroad switchyard to get to her segregated school when there was a white elementary school only four blocks from her home—and it wasn't full. As sensible as it seemed for her to enroll in the white school, Linda was refused admission, despite her qualifications—because she was black.

The pain of that refusal angered and motivated Mr. Brown. He contacted Topeka's National Association for the Advancement of Colored People and asked what could be done. The NAACP had long wanted to challenge segregation in public schools. Linda Brown was the right person at the right time.

The NAACP lawyers requested an injunction to forbid the segregation of Topeka's public schools. It was turned down in the local court. The request arrived at the Supreme Court in 1951. Although there had been other injunctions forbidding segregation, Linda had aroused a nation's sense of guilt in a way no other case before hers had. Injustice was being done to a little girl who wanted and should have a good education.

The librarian drove past wetlands that I had looked forward to seeing, but I let them slip by as green blurs. I was thinking about the question on all of our minds now that we knew desegregation must happen—how long should the states be given to integrate?

I was a product of "white" blindness even at that late date. I thought we should integrate slowly. A captive of my culture and race, I was as slow to see this injustice as a bear awakening from hibernation. Bears awake in steps. First comes a sigh, next a series of soft, low growls, and then slowly, slowly they get to their feet and are on their way—unless they are threatened by an enemy, when a mechanism for survival clicks on. Suddenly the slow heartbeat of dormancy shoots up to normal and the bear is wide awake and running.

I did not emit that first waking sigh until 1932. I was in junior high school in Washington, D.C., the nation's capital and home to the most rigid segregation laws in the nation. I was with the principal of my junior high school, Bertie Bacchus. We were on our way to the Negro school just over the hill from our handsome new school. As I recall, we were going to pick up a sixth grader's prizewinning poem to print in our school newspaper. I was one of the editors at the time and was happy to be chosen to go on a mission with our much loved principal, no matter what she had in mind.

As we reached the top of a rise, I looked down on a neglected building. A brace held up the roof over the entrance. Most of the paint had peeled away. There were no tennis courts or football fields, just clay. I had never seen this school before, although it was only a quarter of a mile from our junior high. Such was the thoroughness of segregation in Washington, D.C.

"Someday this will end," Bertie Bacchus said. I looked to see what would end, and, not seeing, asked.

"Segregation will end," she answered. "These children should be in our school getting as good an education as you are. Right now they're not." Before I could think about that, she added with deep feeling, "Segregation is demeaning and blocks learning."

We entered the school, and Ms. Bacchus tapped on a classroom door.

When it opened, I looked into an unpainted room where kids still hung their clothes on hooks. Plaster had fallen off one wall and the lights were bare bulbs hanging from the ceiling. I don't remember seeing books. A child excused herself from the room and slipped by us, head down, eyes focused on the floor. Later I learned she was on her way to the outhouse.

After graduating from high school. I went to Penn State University, where black students had always been admitted. My black friends had gone to integrated elementary and high schools in Pennsylvania and were interested in the same things I was. We worked for the same ideals on the literary magazine, on reports, on the modern dance floor. It became apparent to me what an equal education meant, and I growled softly as my eyes saw a little light.

At Penn State I studied English and science—I loved to write and my best writing was about ecology, my family profession.

Shortly after graduation World War II broke out. I left my fall term at graduate school and returned to Washington, D.C., to become a newspaper reporter. Men were being drafted and for the first time the newspaper business was obliged, if reluctantly, to hire women.

Occasionally I heard the voices of African American protesters coming from below the Mason-Dixon line, but my concerns were Hitler, food shortages, and battles on far-flung deserts and beaches.

More men were drafted, and I was assigned to Capitol Hill. I took the bus up Pennsylvania Avenue, circled behind the Supreme Court building and got off at the edge of the black ghetto. My brothers and I had often come here as high school students on our trips to the nearby Library of Congress to read about falconry or early settlers.

It was as if I had never seen this place before. I saw not "happy Negroes," as we rationalized them to be, but damaged people. Defeat was written on their faces. Their slumped postures and the poverty they lived in said they had given up. Segregation tore open the soul of this nation right in the shadow of the capitol of the United States. I was ashamed, but not yet aware that something could be done about it.

The war ended. I married and lived in a tent in

a Michigan forest studying the natural history of a farm, helping my husband with the research for his Ph.D. thesis for the University of Michigan. I did not hear the arguments for and against desegregation debated before the Supreme Court. The glorious circumstances of forest and stars surrounding me, and owls calling at night, had lulled me back to sleep.

The librarian drove on. The North Carolina coastal region gave way to the Piedmont area, where American crossbills and redleg salamanders live. I was not looking for them. We were three miles from the librarian's hometown, and I was thinking about what I would say to the children.

The music on the radio stopped, and the news anchor came on.

"The Supreme Court has ordered the desegregation of schools, 'forthwith.'"

The librarian sat upright in her seat.

"That's what we needed," she said, her face blooming like a Japanese water flower. "The Supreme Court has ordered it. We'll do it."

"When?" I asked. She glanced at me.

"Now," she answered. "The Court said 'forthwith.' That means now, today."

"I wish," I said hopelessly.

I do not remember what I said to the children at the library that day, but I do remember the children. All were Caucasian but two. There in the front row, pressed close to the librarian, sat two attentive black children.

Now it is June 2002. To me, the school librarian began the healing those fifty years ago, but as I am shaken awake I see how much must still be done. When?

Today!

JEAN CRAIGHEAD GEORGE received the Newbery Medal for *Julie of the Wolves*. She is the author of several other popular books, including *Julie*, *Julie's Wolf Pack*, and *My Side of the Mountain*.

MY DEAR COLORED PEOPLE

by Leona Nicholas Welch

"MY DEAR colored people . . ." The words resounded, echoing through the downtown cathedral, bouncing from the gold dome to the brass chandeliers and stained-glass windows, to the green-and-gray marble baptismal font, and back to where the bishop stood, clearing his throat for his annual colored graduation oration.

He stood before us, his royal purple, gold, and red robe announcing his right to be there, his jeweled miter proclaiming our privilege to have him there. The white bishop tolerantly addressed us, the graduating students of the only Catholic colored high school in the city, on the one occasion

of the year that we were given free access to the cathedral and the choice of any seat, even those in front. The white Catholics generally steered clear of the cathedral that day. The coloreds would all be there.

It was before the black civil rights marches, sit-ins, and boycotts. It was pre—King and Rosa Parks. It was still "colored" water fountains and dingy, urine-stenched "colored" Greyhound waiting rooms. There was little, if any, talk about mixing schools to fit racial ratios, and most assuredly not by the bishop. True, he had come to confirm that we had reached a landmark, yet he was bound by a personal and Southern-bred commitment to let us know that, though we were completing the main leg of our education, we were still missing the mark on human completeness. We were "dear," but only insofar as our color would allow. Within the confines of the social and political norms of the day, the bishop's expression of "dearness" could only be understood as an expression of the moment. The music of "Pomp and Circumstance" called for at least a whimsical connection between him and his colored diocesan charges.

We stood proud and erect that warm Alabama

Sunday afternoon: the girls, lovely, wrapped in the clean scent of Posners hair pomade and fresh-pressed hair; the boys beaming, hair cut close, brushed to a Duke Pomade-and-water slick finish. Black robes for the boys and white robes for the girls were temporary covers for brand-new gabardine suits and organdy and taffeta dresses, later to be shown off at various parties and dinners.

"My dear colored people . . ." The words, rehearsed year after year, shot from the speaker's mouth in rapid succession. We, the targets, stood rebuffing their deadly impact with the pride and anticipation of diplomas soon to be ours. We would not allow the words to reach our hearts.

Though the temperature in the cathedral was cool, and though the pews (especially designed for white churchgoers) were well proportioned, I found myself fidgeting, my mind moving in and out of the bishop's talk. Now and then my thoughts would drift. The scattered, controlled applause would jolt me back to the gold dome and the white bishop's tirade on what it meant to be colored in our time.

"For the rest of your lives you will thank your teachers and your parents for preparing you to live in *your* world, and to bring forth a living by the power of your own hands." Right at the edge of the word *hands* I felt a powerful urge to get up and walk. I didn't know where I wanted to go or what I would do when I got there. I just needed to move.

"You do not have to go outside the boundaries of your own communities to find new horizons." The bishop's words seemed to shoot like bullets from his mouth and ricochet off the walls, shattering the stained-glass windows, which crashed into a million tiny pieces right inside my chest. My mind drifted. That pressing urge to get up and walk, or even run, tugged at me again, this time more compellingly. I had to take aim against the barrage of words being hurled at my classmates and me. The heat from the bishop's words burned in my head, and I seemed caught up in a cloud of smoke.

In an instant, I felt myself climbing carefully over the feet and laps of the other students in my row. Slowly and deliberately, I walked to the back of the cathedral toward the door. "And my dear colored people . . ." The bishop was still firing his calculated arsenal of words at us. Self-enthralled and immersed in his own noble and generous serving of "new horizons" for coloreds, he paid no attention to me. A deadly hush fell over the audience of mamas and daddies, grandmamas and granddaddies, god-mamas and goddaddies, big mamas and play mamas, uncles, aunts, cousins, and neighbors, all watching and following me with their eyes.

Suddenly from nowhere, off in a distance, I could hear the slow and steady beat of a drum. It seemed to be coming from the direction of the Mobile Bay, as the cathedral was but a few miles from the Bay and the famous Bankhead Tunnel. Without instructions from me, my feet took up the beat of the drums, and I lifted them high as I marched to the back of the church.

By the time I reached the door, I heard a quiet but definite rustle behind me, and somehow I knew that my classmates had chosen to get up and follow me. They knew, without a word passed between us, why I had begun to walk; not to the front to receive a diploma, but to the back. We had heard enough. In single file, the graduating class paraded out through the great oak door, down the steps, and into the sun-lit street.

"Leona Maria Nicholas." The booming, dutiful voice of the bishop broke through my reverie, and had me on my feet in a second. Though still in time with that distant drummer, I was aware of the eyes of those who had worked so hard to bring me to this day. I felt the eyes of my parents, grandmother, sisters, brothers, and friends, loving and proud, carrying me up the cathedral aisle, urging me forward, as they had urged me forward all my life.

Somewhere in a corner of my mind, the instruments of my imagined sunlit street parade caused my head to move and raise itself to a prideful tilt. What had been invested in me by my family warranted this reward. I saw the pride on my parents' faces—a pride collected and saved up just for this day. It would not go to waste. My reverie required one kind of defiance. The love on their faces required yet another.

As I approached the podium, the bishop's earlier words seemed caught somewhere between his jeweled miter and the gold dome of the cathedral. The word *colored,* by the bishop's definition, need not paint our lives. Indeed, by our own definition we were *dear colored people*, and the colors were the same as the love that our families and friends had for us. This love was deep, dark, rich, and flowing. In endless shades, it spilled over into any horizon we desired. And so it was that we were able to spread dignity in the face of indignity. Dignity cannot really be taken away by someone else's poor choice of words.

One by one we filed up to receive our diplomas. *My dear colored people.* We could now dance these words and sing them at the top of our lungs, hearing them echo from downtown Mobile through the tunnel and out into the great Mobile Bay. We could bellow them in our own terms, over the familiar cadences of "Pomp and Circumstance." Yes, we could drum-major and high-step them into our new horizons. Saturated in the sweet power of our own definition, we could parade them—*dear colored people*—up and down every downtown street of white Mobile, crossing over to Davis Avenue and the colored side of town, rocking words in syncopation of our own heartbeats, keeping perfect time with our dreams.

The bishop had come to remind us of what color we were. In actuality, he had only given us the impetus we needed to go show the world our *true* colors.

LEONA NICHOLAS WELCH's first book of poetry, *Black Gibraltar,* received the California Association of Teachers of English award. She is the author of plays, essays, and a novel for children.